Rooted and Winged

poems by

Luanne Castle

Finishing Line Press
Georgetown, Kentucky

Rooted and Winged

Copyright © 2022 by Luanne Castle
ISBN 978-1-64662-863-6 First Edition
All rights reserved under International and Pan-American Copyright Conventions. No part of this book may be reproduced in any manner whatsoever without written permission from the publisher, except in the case of brief quotations embodied in critical articles and reviews.

ACKNOWLEDGMENTS

Verse-Virtual: Your Foot Bone Connected to Your Heart Bone
Saranac Review: Spotlight; April Things
Moonstone's Anthology for Earth Day: The Purpose of Earth
The Orchards Poetry Journal: Without Flight
Anti-Heroin Chic: Into Pulp
Coastal Shelf: The Shape of Me
Humana Obscura: Superbloom
Praxis Magazine: The Rule
Sleet Magazine: How They Fall
MockingHeart Review: When I'm in Charge
Zingara Poetry Review: Finally Going to Tell You about the Staircase Ghost; Maybe It was Spring
Superstition Review: One of Her Parents was a Float
Entropy: Noah and the Middle School Marching Band
Plath Poetry Project: For an Adopted Child; Near
Thimble: Behold the Needle
OPEN:A Journal of A &L: Waterland; Imagine This Portrait
Nine Muses Poetry: Tuesday Afternoon at Magpie's Grill
Red River Review: Why We Wait for Rain
American Journal of Poetry: How to Create a Family Myth
The Practicing Poet: Finding the House on Trimble Street
Linden Avenue: Today and Today and Today

Publisher: Leah Huete de Maines
Editor: Christen Kincaid
Cover Art: Leonard Cowgill
Author Photo: Marisha Castle
Cover Design: Elizabeth Maines McCleavy

Order online: www.finishinglinepress.com
        also available on amazon.com

Author inquiries and mail orders:
Finishing Line Press
P. O. Box 1626
Georgetown, Kentucky 40324
U. S. A.

Table of Contents

I

Tuesday Afternoon at Magpie's Grill 1
How to Create a Family Myth 2
The Shape of Me 3
Waterland 4
Call Me 5
Puzzles and Passages 6
Finding the House on Trimble Street 7
Maybe It Was Spring 8
Your Foot Bone Connected to Your Heart Bone 9
The Box 10
Gravity 11

II

Behold the Needle 15
April Things 16
Noah and the Middle School Marching Band 17
Superbloom 18
The Wildlife Photographer and the Big Kill 19
Javelina Life Rules 20
Big 21
Near 22
Eurydice 23
Why We Wait for Rain 24

III

Into Pulp 27
Self-Portrait as Elegy 28
I Started to Write a Poem about Packing 29

Finally Going to Tell You about the Staircase Ghost 31
One of Her Parents was a Float 32
For an Adopted Child 33
Imagine This Portrait 34
A Year in Bed, with Window 35
When I'm in Charge 36

IV
The Freeze 39
The Risk is That Nothing Changes 40
Hearing Aids 41
The Rule 42
Glass in Glass Behind Glass 43
Today and Today and Today 44
Seekers 45
Meditation 46
Metamorphosis 47
The Purpose of Earth 48
Without Flight 49
How They Fall 50
Spotlight 51
After Darkness 52

NOTES 53

What springs from earth dissolves to earth again, and heaven-born things fly to their native seat.
　　—*Marcus Aurelius*

I

Tuesday Afternoon at Magpie's Grill

Flickering afternoon light slatted and parsed.
At 3PM, the booths empty except for me
and my notebook.
Would I notice if not for my companion,
my need to recognize and remember?
Without a record, will I hear the ice crashing
into the sink, the Dodger talk at the bar
at the end of the room under the Miller Lite
neon confident and beckoning?
My mother used to say about me,
In one ear and out the other, as if the words
flowed through me without stopping,
without truly entering me, leaving little
effect, as if I had no memory
of all the little parental transgressions.
Why am I not under the sycamore I spot
through the blinds in this Tuesday sunshine
listening to the very song with the shady tree?
What have I done with my life? When
I should have written a poem, I didn't.
When I did, I didn't get it quite right.
How can a poem do so many things:
wishing for the shade and thirsty for a beer,
feeling an urge to move my pen and noting
the tiny feet and brush of cuticle,
the solitary fly on my bare arm, while
imagining the chattering of the birds that swoop
from sycamore to jacaranda as if the parking lot
and dumpsters and broken bottles don't exist.
No matter what I notice,
no matter what I record, I will never
capture the ease of wind-filled wings,
tail feathers a translucent backlit fan,
as my hollow bones jettison the detritus
to fly upward against the source.

How to Create a Family Myth

My grandfather built a city with his tongue. Houses and little shops, celery fields and sand lots all connected to each other without roads or sidewalks. Once or twice he showed me a map of sewer lines running like Arcadia Creek underneath the cobblestones and packed dirt. We stood outside and found tall buildings in the clouds overhead. His hands gestured how his grandfather placed the bricks and taught his men to shape upwards, each building higher than the one before. Out there on the stoop, he pointed out where his mother, the one he said I looked like, had witnessed a man beating his horse. I saw her calico skirt billow out behind her, her hands wiping across her apron stomach even as she ran. When she reached the man, she snatched the whip from his hand, his surprise at her actions slowing him, rendering him stupid. When she cracked the whip down on his back time did not go on for her as it did for the rest of the world. Not until a week later, when she went to the market, did she realize that the story ran, too. It kept running until it reached all of us, each child and grandchild and great grandchild taking just what is needed from the tale. In my case, I plucked a heart from the clouds and tucked it safely inside a brick house in the city where it keeps the city alive to this day.

The Shape of Me

Have I been removed from something bigger?
Something gargantuan with jiggerfish capabilities.
Some thing that attracts, precise and cold.
Looking around, I notice cars and trashcans,
and up, clouds suspended in a blue crisp enough to lick.
Can these be my home ship, my grape bunch?
Perhaps they have been sent packing, too, and we all
sit here without motor or navigation and stunned.
I'll wait with the emptied soup cans and stubs. Or.
Put me back where I fit just to prove there is such.
It is possible that I have been discarded from small.
So small that all my ghosts and angels become each
other and then me with a hinted outline of wings.
No, leave me here where I am unknown but solid.

Waterland

In the b&w my mother stands on the steep lakeshore,
her back to the tall weeds and the turbid water below.
The newborn in her arms, face posed to the lens,
is me. I've done my best with feet and fists, my small
lungs blossoming like paper flowers in water, but she
is young and healthy and survived the assault of my birth.

A creative region, the water below mute and protective
with invisible hatchings of suckers, perch, of bullfrogs, but
for the silent snake undulating on the surface like Jesus,
like me dancing in levitation without pointe shoes.
The snake and me and Jesus, but first I was in her arms
and young and healthy and survived my own birth.

They found Jesus in the pillars, in the nebula where
born of cold and gas and dust and shrinking and breaking
apart the clouds, the protostar kills its parent to live.
After scaring away Jesus, more infant stars force gas jets
to discharge bombettes and comets, the fireworks' finale,
and the new star, young and healthy, survives its birth.

Reflected in the lake below, the stars watch their lives.
Their light glints off the snake's prismatic varied scales
and the bullfrogs' yellow throats along the weedy shore.
Bluegills snap up larvae in slivers of illusory light.
Stars and snakes and frogs and fish, infants and mothers,
forever young and healthy here, survive their lives.

Call Me

You thought I was created to whisk
at your feet as you ran in your clumsy
orange life jacket, chubby toes clutching the sand,
my waters passing over and between before
I coaxed back in a fort-da flirt, your parents
chittering nervously nearby. You thought
me an ocean, the sky, the end of Earth,
and as flashback, a crone rocking the cradle.
Only I remember the name of the mound-
builders, their math in copper and teeth. They
in turn knew my second name, not the true one
from my ice mother when she poured me
into the aching and flawed flanks of land.
I know your name and all who came before you.

Puzzles and Passages

Hide a letter in plain sight, in the spaces
between the others. Make it an I to demonstrate
your frustration or a C to make a metaphor.
It doesn't matter. Nothing will be solved.
We're trained to notice lines and curves, not
their absence, the hole inside. Until we find
it's a way out, we don't see. We embrace
illusions. Take where I grew up, inside
the carefully connected dots of four lakes.
With my assorted pencils I colored Michigan
the most vibrant variation, Superior sky blue,
Huron pearl gray, and Erie emerald. Then
yellow, orange, red, and purple, a tornado
of drama. We colored them anew for five days
as memory exercise. But inside those waters
lapping at me on the shore, welling up on
my plastic shovel, pulling me out deep, I didn't
notice the aperture, no, passage between them.

Finding the House on Trimble Street

The house, once white and raw, has matured into gold. Ripened maples in October red temptingly frame the remembrance. The garage neatly unfolds from the side, the lawn edged in definition. You imagine responsible owners, their unblemished lives. They don't know who stacked cement blocks into a basement bunker. A girl slept above the so-called shelter, and when the sirens roared, her parents brought her downstairs into the dank cave. Sometimes it was a tornado with its green sky, and sometimes it was a bomb with its puff of smoke and a white rabbit in the magician's hat. When she played outside in the woods behind the house, she watched the color of the sky for changes—pink, purple, chartreuse. In the grass, she looked for a four-leaf clover, but never found it. She crouched to examine helpless red worms on the sidewalk in front, searching for a nightcrawler or a bloodworm that bites. At night she lay awake for hours in her small bed, listening for the plinky-plink on the roof. Or the solitary train whistle from the nearby tracks.

>   freight train passes by
>   taking time and distance
>   leaving memories

Maybe It was Spring

or winter
and there were nine girls or seven.
Certainly it was overnight church camp
when we formed a second
skin around Lacy
with our fingertips.
What happened wasn't a dream unless
a mass dream dreamed en masse.
We were one organism,
the skin we made stretched
tautly like a drumhead, lifting
up the girl Lacy, a musical offering.
Our song flowed in and from us,
all seven or nine, with Lacy the melody.
But one of us must have felt an itch
and discovered she was separate
and, doing so, withdrew her touch.
An epidemic followed
from this undoing until Lacy's body
shared many points
of contact with the floor.
I remember looking under her
just before and noting
her two inches above it all
though of course that is ridiculous
because it wasn't a dream.

Your Foot Bone Connected to Your Heart Bone

Afternoons that unspool, weaving extra hours
between lunch crumbs and dinner prep,
the air in the screened front porch crisp
as a newly plucked apple, the old rocker
the woman with the girl cradled in her lap
as if the universe begins from there,
the dry fat fingers around the girl's feet
and of course the foot bone connected
to the heel bone, tickle tickle giggle giggle
and their voices harmonize dem bones
dem bones, dem dry bones, hear the word.
Being the daughter of a daughter, the girl
formed first in the grandmother, one
of many explanations for their bond.
She taught her to feed the possums
and crows and accept the gifts they left
in gratitude. Stones, feathers, skulls.
On afternoons like today the pungent decay
damp leaves too long now on the ground
a reluctance to move forward except
to rock steadily staring at her own damn feet.

The Box

I'm folding you, smoothing so you lie flat
and Grandpa, too. What can I do?
Next that blue! new to me I brought you
with sureness to hatch, your magic so potent.
A red leaf in the shape of the mother tree.
I helped you pack this lunchbox for our walk
down the block, call him up from the pit.
The lunchbox meant to hold a thermos,
looks like a plastic coffin, makes a lump.
These layers must ring each one the next.
If slashed through, the concentric circles
would emit essences and confused ghosts.
Rather than carry packages loose, dropping
and retrieving, merely a vaudevillian fool.
What I mean is that I am a good traveler,
filling my shoes with sock balls & panties.
I'm seeing it all from the inside so self-
absorbed. The curious might check for their
own dead; others set it out by the trash cans.

Gravity

Why are we only of the earth, Grandpa?
See your knees sunken in muck,
the sun sketching every plane of you.

You balance a new potato in your palm,
ask me to decide if we dig now or let
them stay buried to toughen up.

Even before us, they plowed fields
and sewed leather onto soles, their lives
spun from the loom beneath them.

We could puff into the blue like clouds.
Why hasn't one of us learned to fly?
What keeps us pointed downward?

Your mother dug in her heels to birth
you in the house her father built
on fertile city land he saved for.

Did you ever yearn to fly, Grandpa?
Can you buy sky the way you sink
into the dirt you were born in?

Where do you hoist a flag or hold
still to hug your grandchildren?
How could I be that free?

II

Behold the Needle

I hold between my fingers
its lack of suitability for this task
to take apart the earth beneath me
for the memories grow together
like moldy pages, impossible
to separate: the celery fields,
striped black and green, July 4
corn and purple chicory, salted
sand of San Diego, lit ribbons
of LA traffic, twin downtowns
still climbing over Phoenix's
saguaro-studded sun-splayed
hills, the dark lake waters that
lap and lick the weedy shore.
When I most need to accept
I cannot be only here and not
there and there at the same time:
thus the needle to pry the places
apart, but the way needles are
is that they travel in and out,
knotting as they move about.

April Things

If you spot two birds of prey in one day
different roads different angle of the sun
both with beaks glutted with hearts
gizzards, spindly legs dangling
it means something beyond dinner or death
or that it's April or the cataclysm
but some thing to the framer or the eye
quickened by the sight.
As the first arcs overhead, a hawk clutching
a lizard, another lizard just beyond the wire
fence scoots a rock aside, a saguaro's top
blossom grins toward the sun, a man
too big and idle in a driverless sedan picks
his nose and glances furtively aside as
a truck spins out, fire erupting from its guts.
Nostrils flare and farther on, on
another highway, the sky is clear and no
thing in view. Later, broad black wings
sweep the sky in linear fashion, a soft
white bundle hanging from its clench.
More than shape or color, the movement
of weight and substance—a hint of alive
drapes the mind as wisteria pregnant
with blossoms hang from the beams.

Noah and the Middle School Marching Band

It is green and blue and yellow where
I can see out the window
instead of concentrating on the page.
That famous poet chastised me
for putting birds in poems
as if he released them from
their lined and stanzaed cages when
he grew bored with their singing.
But you know what? I'm alone
with my paper and who will care
if I lure them in with my baton-
like pen, parading them into place
two by two like Noah and the
middle school marching band.
It's not just robins and wrens.
Look at them come. Godwits
and bushtits, catbirds and black-
crested titmice, I tickle their feet
to move them along a little faster.
Come on, coots and loons with
the juncos and cuckoos, the dippers,
the pink-footed shearwaters.
Watch for the yellow legs,
the redstarts, bespeckled ovenbirds.
Quails and rails, pintails and pewees.
Now watch my favorites, most social
of them all, chattery magpies.
Inside my shabby bars, they wobble
on perches I improvise as they arrive.

Superbloom

On my big brown mountains
are rocks
that grow larger
though not visibly
also lichen, sow thistle, bristle grass
without water you can smell.

One bird seeks a saguaro
like a mast on a masklike sea
rabbits and voles above and below
my skin
run through chaparral.

All is brown or turning brown
crisp, nearly weightless as tumbleweed
waiting for the first spark
a catch like the charge of the first nucleus
flame-thunder rolls
all is black, charred, a false wall.

When the rains dampen
the animals are smoked from their secrets
deluge covers like an ocean
they call it disaster
It is the time before the asters

the lupine, filaree, and monkeyflower
desert paintbrush, ocotillo, cactus flowers
brittle bush, creosote, bladder pod
and when the calamities are particularly ripe
fulsome fields of golden poppies.

The Wildlife Photographer and The Big Kill

Two months of this desert fever. I linger on the couch with my elderly cat. We are both still and silent, me plotting where I live from here, she lost in exhaustion. A quick movement past the window, I observe a cottontail nibbling, its onyx eyes darting in automaton-fashion, nose working. It's all tucked into itself, and yet splays its senses all about, alert for hunters, probability set against its survival to maturity. At frame's edge, a shift of the wind perhaps, but enough to change my perspective and spot a bobcat blending with the copse in its predator stance crouch, motionless, patient to pounce. Do I have time to rise, run to the door, and shout? Vulnerability must be protected at all costs. At the handle, I pause. Through the door pane I'm now closer to the wild cat with its stoical hunger. The rabbit is out of view. A hemisphere of mind peels away. What's left is raw and untroubled.

Javelina Life Rules

Only eat meat if it's going to waste
Stick to a varied diet that grows
from the land under your hooves.
Pick your way carefully, so's not
to trample your salad fixings.
Move along the wash to stay close
to humans for their chewy verbena,
their spring-tender shoots and small
pots of cactus. You will find water
and juice-plump leaves this way.
Choose a mesquite tree to sleep
under; be framed by your family.
Don't let your bare snout burn.
Look out for bobcats and coyotes,
even more, those that smell human—
their manic lunges and threat-shouts.

Big

You said our animals are in danger from it. Guard the doors so our civilized cats don't in their naiveté fall prey to an early morning shadow of themselves. The shock of adjusting my vision to a stranger on my property as if an unwashed man roams our wash, come from under the overpass, eyes a windfall on his way down river. In this dry season the river is invisible, but paces ahead. This is no man. His—though why he's male I can only sense, but is it my sense or his?—ungroomed ruff and dusty coat, his barroom stare. As if he sprang full grown from the dirt and hungry, he alone in a primeval solitude. He takes me in and discards me as so much gristle. He's tall as my car hood. He can grip a lesser cat. The cats that curl next to me and each other on the couch. That purr at my touch. I could find a club or rock in the garage or out back, if necessary. Then this crouching thing inside me takes flight with a whoosh of broad wings, eager to share in the stranger's gluttony of the land down the wash.

Near

In the small shade it crouches
and on the glistening leafy crown,
in the crotch of the mesquite under
the stray songbird Mexico-bound.

It glides at the base of the stiff
yellow grasses like desert snakes.
Within heat shimmers, tiny moving
rainbow mirage, the racing light.

It pants, splayed, and when I go
inside and press my face to glass,
it humps vacantly, then watch:
a wink tossed my way, the demon.

I do not wonder at it even when
I spy it scuttling under my bed
or dead and desiccated among
my mother's creams and brushes.

It spreads over my skin, in fact,
as if a balm in the arid air.
When I cut my chicken breast fine
it rides the knife. I could choke.

It lives in the desert.
But also the pastures and pavement,
the seas and the Technicolor mountains.
There is no running from it.

It is whatever you want it to be,
but always what you most fear.
Hear the banging of the pans, the spoons?
Smell the creosote? Rain has arrived.

Eurydice

I couldn't open my eyes this morning, although I tried to flip up my lids with my forehead and temple muscles. Because my tongue was stuck to the roof of my mouth, I made my way to the faucet where I poured and drank a glass of water, all the while worrying that without opening my eyes my hearing would sharpen and I would hear things I don't want to know. My roommate examined my eyes and discovered a spider web inextricably woven into both sets of lashes. I had reason for concern. The hairs on my arms vibrated to cries of the violin across town, and I began to walk the fourteen miles without a white cane. Traffic surged around me, although it created a wind to flirt with my skirt. I felt it, but of course could not see the intent. When I approached my destination, the music slowed into an absolute silence. Then came the crashing of the violin upon the rocks.

Why We Wait for Rain

We wait for hours watching the dark unfurling
toward us, unsure
if it will land here at all

whether it carries thunderstorm or haboob

It smells like rain
bittersweet cocktail of sandstone & blossoms
still damp and quickening in the air

over ten thousand years

It's why we wait for rain
tornadoes of dust don't set off the scent
a drizzle dampening its branches

awakens the languishing senses

We wait to run through wet branches and shake
drops from our shoulders, caught
in the sharp unmistakable fragrance

wanting it to pool inside us in reservoir

III

Into Pulp

Lakewater pushes at my ankles
toes slicing an evanescent path
I'm at an age where I think *I'm at the age*
and I don't imagine eyerolls
where I sense time abrading my surface
like this constantly moving water
stones and minnows distort into segments
molecules into a variety of atomic individuals
two purple, no, one hairbrush, a plastic ball
a swaying branch, leaves decaying
the insides of my grandmothers' fridges
bubble and pop into shards of memory
dangerous to the touch though I do still see
one packed and one bare but for
spoiled milk and insulin bottles.
Even if I don't move the water sways
so I feel it undulating a vintage possibly
familiar scene, aluminum-sided
backdrop with foundation plantings trimmed
with lattice, a lawn to mow, a couple
long since gone, he a Great War vet
You can see—I can see—she has to make all
the decisions for them, crisp in
white polyester pants, a painted
smile, though it's hard to be sure through
the water's movement over and back
it's been so long since I've seen these two
perhaps we have known each other
somewhere as the edges of time
have curled; if I haul memory from this grave
the transmigration into pulp continues

Self-Portrait as Elegy

An electric ship holds still
at the edge of sea. Hasten. Observe.
Nothing moves but its own glow,
yet it cannot be caught or boarded.
They say even now it sends
messages to captains and skippers
dead before you and I were born.
But what does it wish to convey?
A vessel may travel a long time
on dreams and speculative histories.
It's so hard to let go of self-plans.
What we have here is a portent
or a moment to watch our lives slip
past, leaving us agape on the deck.

I Started to Write a Poem about Packing

My question involves the location of beauty in each moment.
It's what happens to me in the waking up moment
and the teeth brushing ones.
Like how the tuning fork of the limbs starts going
when you're slipping on your work shoes
and you hear the spheres sing so you
call in sick.
It might be harmony or symmetry.
Syncopation with the startling or odd.

My question chases its own tail until I am chattering
with a timid ferocity.
A question isn't for answering, but for asking,
and my question knows that but wants
the gratis pretty misting down and welling up:
the alluring way the plastic bag swirls
around the tree trunk, another balances
from the branches.
The fetching rain clouds swell violet.
How does it happen that gray is now flowers and grapes?
That a broken bottle separates light into many reds,
blues, yellows, greens? A sliver of purple in one.
If you didn't call in sick, paint your self-portrait
with pushpins. Dance on your desk.
Can you see it? Touch it? Hear the purity.

It's the most important question anyone has ever asked.
No other question comes close to giving me
a reason to go to work or run away.
How to handle a question that insinuates
itself in every second of our lives?
Is beauty here? There? When you try to pin
a definition on it, meaning dissipates into
a thousand blinking fireflies.
It could be the golden egg. Accept it or it's your loss.
If you read the title, you know I am packing for a journey,
rolling shirts to fit into corners and searching

for my umbrella, just in case. But in the mundane
I'm imagining something splendid. My suitcase
filled with magic cards and baklava.

Finally Going to Tell You about the Staircase Ghost

When my baby said *peaches, peaches,*
I put the can into the opener.
Its lid rose on the machine's arm.
The peaches smelled peachy-spice
and curled into little moons.
My son gummed his peaches, sloshing
juice from his mouth's ends.
I washed out the can and then saw
what I had missed in my loving him
like water into wine. The cool blond
of pear slices on the Del Monte label.
The membrane between here
and there can separate as an unexpected
wind swishes silk draperies apart.

Here's another one.
You might not have noticed.
You could have been standing
at the base of the stairs,
seen a woman in a long shift hesitate.
What was happening was this.
My foot reached for the next step,
and in that instant a ghost
passed through my chest
on its way downstairs. It didn't
move out of the way for me,
didn't care that I knew it existed.
We both went our separate ways,
my path leading me to this moment
where I tell my tiny limitless tales.

One of Her Parents was a Float,

the other an underwater island.
One parent was a circulating library,
the other a television signal.
Across the ocean, other parents
read a language like a movie.
In the dawn, one parent collected
hearts, while the other meant
to fertilize daisies and milkweed.
Somewhere other parents were
a teapot and a shovelful of clay.
One parent was a blackberry bramble,
the other a signed Bible missing pages.
Still others were buses, candles, pickles,
and empty strollers. She felt confused.
One parent gave a palm to land on,
another gave a velvet couch cushion,
yet another a musical note. One held
an unwrapped gift for wondering over.

For an Adopted Child

You will grow a new set of feelings, eventually,
a braided tree trunk, like a ficus, that supports a bloom
of love, shame, and sadness, fruit of flower & wasp—
a trapping pit when the branches give way, decay
behind a madonna mask, dark spots cast by our lamp.

But right now the hand under your head,
whispered kisses—you don't see behind them,
sensing the fullness within and stable gravity
without, it's all so seamless, tightly swaddled
almost —your dimpled new smile mirrors mine.

I wrinkle my nose, you squeeze your face.
One day you will see us together and understand
the warning you have heard your whole life
about the missing—until then let's feed on these figs.

Imagine This Portrait

Think of him as the ice she slid on
  to the center of the world
And the worldly air she projected
  during games of deep concentration.
Think of him as buried deep inside
  with a heart covered only by membrane
And the hat that slips between us and God
  to cover our sins and wisecracking.
Think of him as the crack in the counter
  we fill with goo and cure with heat.
Think of him as the heat that fries our skin
  in the two-week cure for wintry blues
And the apple-cured bacon we overcook,
  crumble, and add to everything we eat.
He's the addition to everything she is
  and the frosty fire pink of her fine eye.

A Year in Bed, with Window

Within the bed's borders
a small table on metal arm
drapes over my body
On the table a laptop
open and warm
One cat under my arm
another at my feet
The television in the corner
of the living room
rumbles on hour by hour
but it's too far outside
this bed to make sense
Every day I read pages
about Henry VIII
I'm still on Catherine
and her cancer, hating
her mean husband,
while mine handles kids
and work and pays
the petsitter to make me
omelets for lunches.
They talk and I ignore
them. Billie Holiday
sings *all of me* in my ear
all day long in this bed
that fits me and my cats.
Nothing outside the edges
of the bed matters to me
Not the wind sifting through
the aspen leaves way up
there or the lizard sunning,
a bicyclist's hair streaming
on her way to the market.

When I'm in Charge

Someday you will realize it was me
and know what you've lost.
When the cancer cure is announced,
I will be the anonymous healer.
I will defeat A.I. before it takes over
our world, outwit the hackers,
the scammers and spammers.
You will realize I designed a safe
airbag, cultivated thirty new flavors
of raspberry and pineapple, let
lima beans go extinct. That I wrote
a wildly successful Christmas song.
Like the boy seeing the emperor,
I exposed big lies with one push
of the button, but kept the little ones;
only I knew the difference.
You can thank me for solving
what was known as the gun problem.
We're all safe in the future because
of what I've done, outlawing grief
and its wily predecessor love.

IV

The Freeze

My first memory of a poem was when a sunbeam angled just so.
A silver sword sliced away the afternoon, leaving a haze over the lake.
The poems might have begun in my mother's womb, but the way
the sun came between me and the water will always seem an introduction.
I sat on the shore in my life jacket and carved out of the sand a buried lake.
The glint of the silver blade drew my attention up and the world was new.
They visited me often from then on. The complicated ant living
its complicated life hidden from me by dandelions and flowering clover.
The furry brown caterpillar, with its magician's tricks, performing for us kids.
The day I lay on my back and watched the flick book of clouds changing.
I never thought of trapping the poems, little fish, holding them captive.

The Risk is That Nothing Changes

There in the gravel past the gas company
flag not ten steps from the saguaro
a mist rises from a rabbit hole.
If I put my eye to it will it harden
my vitreous humor or compose my tears?
The vapor grows. A shape develops, no.
Not a shape, but a want stitched from felt
and thin paper, damp with unknown tears.
People trudge past, through the haze
which now reaches across the sidewalk—
small groups of recurring characters bent
under a light drizzle and incompletion.
I know without knowing how I know
that the glow from their ribs means
they have been electrified and live again.
How do I set my dead ones striding here?
Or shall I leave them where they be?
Grandma trimming piecrust, Grandpa pulling
radishes. My father yearning and dissatisfied.

Hearing Aids

My mother ordered hearing aids
which looks strange written since we don't write seeing aids
for glasses, itself an odd one
referring to two chips of plastic once glass
floating in a frame,
the skeleton of a house or boundaries for art
that sets in motion pinning a rap
on innocence,
a wrap that begs rending.
When Koko the gorilla admired her tiara-self in the mirror
the humans had pecked away at hers.
Koko talked like finger bracelet for ring.
A kitten is All Ball.
At her age, my mother is no longer
innocence, but wile in a patched jacket
piecing together sense from
sounds no longer sentences, but ratatat.
My mother is old enough to create
meaning from runtogethersyllables on TV and stage,
from our phone talks. She figures out
what she wants to hear. She pours tea there
and I pour mine here. Our spouts speak the same.

The Rule

It doesn't matter if the boiler
threatens to blow like a demented pianist
and bees mass on the wall
into a Rorschach designed for psychos
and nobody answers the phone and
the room separates into two slightly
offset images that lure you into
the hallway that isn't there
and this morning's nightmare strands
you in a crowded public market
of caged body parts
and the stallkeepers don't wear masks
but still all look identical
and when you turn on the TV
the hole where images should be
bubbles with cockroaches lurching
toward you with their giraffe lopes
and syrup drips down the wallpaper
to feed the rest of the pests
because you still have to stay alone
in your own lonely home so
you outline your feet with yellow paint
on the plank floor so you don't move.

Glass in Glass Behind Glass

With the gold faded,
her hair is now the white
of gown, face, wings,
and praying hands.
White as mine that
grows as if all is right.
Paint hasn't faltered
from the halo aplomb
bragging its emblem.
The glass ball that
housed her diorama
shattered at the hands
of someone careless.
Careless I let him.
Sharp and jagged edges
drew a fine line in red
across my finger
when I palmed her
quick, with great loss.
They saw anyway.
I am a cockroach
in this dusty house.
She lives a butterfly's
life in a jar filled with
glass marbles behind
a glass cabinet door.

Today and Today and Today

Today her bath takes an hour. She hasn't the strength to help you pull her out of the now cool water. Your shoulder and back ache. You should rinse the tub, but she needs help toweling her body—that once strong body now diminished by disease—and seeing it makes you sad. You wrap the gown around her shoulders and button each button for her. She either ignores you or says mean things or praises you endlessly. Each response makes you sad.

Today you have trouble getting his nasal cannula hooked behind his ears and then realize the oxygen tank is almost empty. He complains his mouth is dry, his tongue is dry, his throat is dry. He's cold. Where is his sweater? It seems to have disappeared. He can wear only that one sweater. The others are too thin, too thick, too warm, too prickly, or pull over the head. Now he needs to get to the toilet fast. Once the oxygen tank is hooked to the back of the wheelchair, you help him shift to the chair from the bed. The journey to the bathroom and back will be long and harrowing. And your shoulder again aches.

Today you visit your wife for six hours and then again in the evening for two more. This was yesterday's schedule, and it will be tomorrow's schedule. She lies on the thin mattress and rarely responds to you. But you feel she knows you are at her side, joking with the staff, making sure that aides and nurses alike care for her as they would their mothers because her submissive form has been brushed with the glow of your personality.

Today you show him an old photo album of the two of you when you were young. You point out people and remind him of pleasant times. He says he is dying, and you remind him that he has so much to live for, though at the moment you know it sounds hollow in the face of what he must feel. You keep knives away from him and hope he's forgotten the old revolver in the basement. You don't feel like smiling either, although when you took a walk three days ago and smelled the fresh honeysuckle you found yourself grinning like a fool.

Seekers

They come with their rank breath
when we're desperate for sleep
bleeding into our pores, the folds
and fissures of our brains, suffusing
our lobes with the history of their
scents, the timbre of their voices.
The visuals are brief, jump cut,
mistaken. They might be sincere.
Their superpowers allow them
to make cameos in our dreams
appear inside the lock, deadbolt,
and chain when we're home alone.
They might be the fourth guest
in the delivery room, enveloping
like vernix and lanugo, unlike them.
Everlasting. At loud parties, don't
go in the backyard to see the moon
teetering on the mountaintop
because they watch, waiting for
that moment to slip up behind you.
If you meet them at cemeteries
they won't keep their promises.
They will continue to seek you.

Meditation

Crushed between my thumb
and first finger, the earthy
sharp-sweet odor bursts out.
If I could release my thoughts
like mint, sending them away.
I'll put leaves in iced tea
and inhale deeply as I sip.
But each thought I have
relates to the others, a sort
of oversoul of thinking and
a despot of all that's mental.
Next to the mint, two tiny
peppers progress in calyxes
so dear and most reliable.
And then the basil said to be
more beautiful than oregano.
I'm trying, really trying hard
to form a meditation on plants.
They are not immune to virus,
but these are safe in my garden.
I might be safe in my garden
with my mint-trimmed tea
and herbs for spaghetti sauce.
The thoughts come get me.
They are relentless, insatiable.
My rosemary bush might do
the trick, with its strong scent
and evergreen resilience.

Metamorphosis

The last puffs of the sweet acacia darken and shrink
as their mates circle thickly underneath..

Next-door the icy green branches of the palo verde
quicken into a summer-dress yellow.

A saguaro now wears a hard green cap that will
eventually burst into white blossoms

and the man still marks time by moving his peas
from one pan to another in a rhythm he's determined.

I own a tower of a clock that chimes on the hour
and one on the wall that plays "My Heart Will Go On."

Outside my wooly butterflybush blooms in March
and will overstay the spring pinks and yellows.

One day the mouse ran up the clock and nothing changed.
The saguaro flower still opened and the peas shifted.

My snapdragons and geraniums are spindly; it's time
for summer flowers, the salvias and feathery celosias.

They get their beats from the sun, a monotonous meter.
One emerges from her chrysalis, glistening and small,

red dilates the veins of her wings that swell full-size.
The change that is no change is now complete.

She flies now to the rocking twig of the palo verde,
camouflaging the taps engraved on the sheet music

The Purpose of Earth

What comes from the earth are rocks, worms,
broken frescoes
What goes into the earth can be roots, a pot
of coins, even water though what happens
to it depends
If you put your ear up to it
you'll hear the same
echo found in a seashell or your lover's chest
If you press your bare feet
from where you come they will be
reborn to touch differently than face
or hands
Imagine putting your arms around it
Wish you could make them long enough
Even birds and bats fall to earth when
they die
Golems rumble out of the earth but
we fail to recognize them as we crash
to the ground together

Without Flight

Wildness creeps and slithers and bobs and darts
through the wash. Above, the chitters and caws
are punctuated by fluttering from palo verde
to mesquite. These are the vulnerable.
In the hanging succulent outside the window
two squabs await their mother's return, a beak
clutching grasses and grains. My husband guards
the nest in her absence, cautiously waters roots.

Others follow the map of the wash, searching
for quail, rabbits, young snakes, and lizards.
We've shielded our eyes from the sun to see
two hawks soaring, then circling, and swooping.
Owls stand sentinel at the roof edge. The bobcat
and coyotes target and strike their own prey.
Our tears are for the weak, the quail chick bullied
from the brood, the bunny struggling in the pool.

So when I encounter the red-tail guarding
the dove nest from below, my innards lurch.
Even massive with wings withdrawn, she demands
awe and reservation. She must have eaten one,
readying for the next, but all my window banging
and pan clanging doesn't move her on. I admit
sweat gathers on me. Could be the heat or her.
I consider rushing her to save that last chick.

But I remember hawks heavy winged above me,
the gliding and patterns and power in the sky.
And now she stands on the concrete, motionless,
where she has no more business than a whale
on the beach, and me where I live rooted to earth
observing her unable to ride a thermal to rise fast,
to set her wings and soar on purpose and beyond.
To catch her without flight is the catastrophe.

How They Fall

What falls away is always. And is near.
The doe pressed by fear at cliff edge.
The parachutist who plummets through cloud,
tiny glittering crystals adhere like insects,
dampening her suit and helmet.
Love is hard and away. Being young
and too close to his mother, it was necessity.
The next one, watch her. Falling like float,
the slight whir as she parts the air, her strong
wing bones fanned out, her arm crooked
to push hair from her mouth open without scream—
straight from heaven to earth. I follow
at night as I sleep without landing, my arms
akimbo, hands at my crown, mouth wide.
I'm without voice. See the knobby scars
where the wings once grew as spindles.

Spotlight

Months go by, and I don't recognize the gloaming. Then it's late November again. At this time of day, Grandma used to stand under the bulb over the sink that haloed her and pearlized the onions she chopped. Potatoes and carrots from the root cellar fanned her like a sunburst. Outside, murk enveloped tree branches, porch chair, surrounded the sturdy walls of the little house. Grandma switched on the kitchen light, creating an intimate stage amidst the darkening world. She held my hands in hers to peel a potato. The rhythm of the parer became known to me. The backdoor swung open, and Grandpa, in his greasy Sunoco blues, waved on his way down to the shower head installed above the basement floor drain. Chuck roast seared in the Dutch oven, and the spatters almost drowned out the shower's cascade, but not quite. On his way to the television with bunny ears in the next room, Grandpa picked me up and, mid-air, rubbed noses. I called him a bath baby with whiskers. Then the voices of the TV show, the sizzling of the meat, and Grandma singing *you'll be swell, you'll be great, I can tell, just you wait* made me forget there was darkness elsewhere and ahead. When the day closes up early, best to be in the dark looking up for starlight.

After Darkness

When the last star falls to the others,
it darkens like the hush in a theatre,
a twinkling or two from silence.
It darkens sudden, as when the music
stops and, without its guidance, we stumble.
It darkens like a road to nowhere, an Oslo
afternoon, California when the continent
wraps up for night. It can darken
like an executioner's hood, a lid lowered,
over it all, unexpected blindness.
Watch how the wrong word extinguishes
the light. It darkens like earth under
the vulture's wings, a smudge
that lengthens with time and grief.
Then, long after, a flicker from the pile.
We bring our efforts to the task.

NOTES

The song that informs "Your Foot Bone Connected to Your Heart Bone" is "Dem Bones," written by poet and composer James Weldon Johnson and his brother, J. Rosamond Johnson. My grandmother, inspired by a version by The Delta Rhythm Boys, used to sing it to me when I was on her lap.

"Near" was written for the *Plath Poetry Project*, inspired by Sylvia Plath's "A Birthday Present."

"For an Adopted Child" was written for the *Plath Poetry Project*, inspired by Sylvia Plath's "For a Fatherless Son."

Albert Camus' novel *The Plague* and the image of the man marking time by shifting peas shows up in "Metamorphosis."

The first line of "How They Fall" was borrowed from the Theodore Roethke villanelle, "The Waking."

Luanne Castle's *Kin Types* (Finishing Line Press), a chapbook of poetry and flash nonfiction, was a finalist for the Eric Hoffer Award. Her first collection of poetry, *Doll God*, winner of the New Mexico-Arizona Book Award for Poetry, was published by Aldrich Press. Luanne has been a Fellow at the Center for Ideas and Society at the University of California, Riverside. She studied English and Creative Writing at the University of California, Riverside (PhD); Western Michigan University (MFA); and Stanford University. Her Pushcart and Best of the Net-nominated poetry and prose have appeared in *Copper Nickel, American Journal of Poetry, Pleiades, River Teeth, TAB, Verse Daily, Glass: A Journal of Poetry*, and other journals. An avid blogger, she can be found at luannecastle.com. She lives in Arizona, where she shares land with a bobcat.

CPSIA information can be obtained
at www.ICGtesting.com
Printed in the USA
BVHW040118140922
646955BV00003B/127

9 781646 628636